D1201556

STATE PROFILES

PUERTO RICO

BY ALICIA Z. KLEPEIS

BELLWETHER MEDIA • MINNEAPOLIS, MN

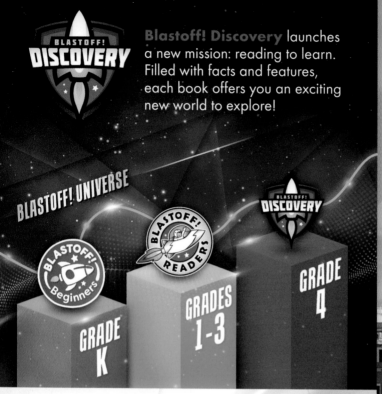

Blastoff! Discovery launches a new mission: reading to learn. Filled with facts and features, each book offers you an exciting new world to explore!

BLASTOFF! UNIVERSE

BLASTOFF! Beginners — GRADE K

BLASTOFF! READERS — GRADES 1-3

BLASTOFF! DISCOVERY — GRADE 4

This edition first published in 2022 by Bellwether Media, Inc.

No part of this publication may be reproduced in whole or in part without written permission of the publisher.
For information regarding permission, write to Bellwether Media, Inc., Attention: Permissions Department,
6012 Blue Circle Drive, Minnetonka, MN 55343.

Library of Congress Cataloging-in-Publication Data

Names: Klepeis, Alicia, 1971- author.
Title: Puerto Rico / by Alicia Z. Klepeis.
Description: Minneapolis, MN : Bellwether Media, Inc., 2022. | Series: Blastoff! Discovery: State profiles | Includes bibliographical references and index. | Audience: Ages 7-13 | Audience: Grades 4-6 | Summary: "Engaging images accompany information about Puerto Rico. The combination of high-interest subject matter and narrative text is intended for students in grades 3 through 8" – Provided by publisher.
Identifiers: LCCN 2021020874 (print) | LCCN 2021020875 (ebook) | ISBN 9781644873441 (library binding) | ISBN 9781648341878 (ebook)
Subjects: LCSH: Puerto Rico–Juvenile literature.
Classification: LCC F1958.3 .K55 2022 (print) | LCC F1958.3 (ebook) | DDC 972.95–dc23
LC record available at https://lccn.loc.gov/2021020874
LC ebook record available at https://lccn.loc.gov/2021020875

Text copyright © 2022 by Bellwether Media, Inc. BLASTOFF! DISCOVERY and associated logos are trademarks and/or registered trademarks of Bellwether Media, Inc.

Editor: Kate Moening   Designer: Laura Sowers

Printed in the United States of America, North Mankato, MN.

TABLE OF CONTENTS

A family arrives at El Yunque National Forest. They head out on the Mount Britton Trail, walking among the trees and crossing rushing streams. In the branches, bright green Puerto Rican todies call to each other.

CASTILLO SAN FELIPE DEL MORRO

CULEBRA NATIONAL WILDLIFE REFUGE

PARQUE DE BOMBAS

PARQUE NACIONAL DE LAS CAVERNAS DEL RÍO CAMUY

The family eats a snack at Mount Britton Tower. The surrounding **rain forest** is every shade of green. In the late afternoon, they check out the Angelito Trail. Ginger plants give off a spicy smell. Before leaving, the children jump off a rope swing into a clear natural pool below. Welcome to Puerto Rico!

Puerto Rico is a United States **territory**. It is located about 1,000 miles (1,609 kilometers) southeast of Florida. The territory sits between Hispaniola and the Virgin Islands. It covers 5,325 square miles (13,792 square kilometers). The Caribbean Sea lies south of Puerto Rico. The Atlantic Ocean borders Puerto Rico's northern shores.

The **commonwealth** of Puerto Rico has over 140 islands. The largest is the rectangular island of Puerto Rico. The capital city of San Juan is on Puerto Rico's northern coast. People also live on Vieques and Culebra. These islands lie to the east.

MONA PASSAGE

THE MONA PASSAGE

The Mona Passage is a body of water between Puerto Rico and the Dominican Republic. Many boats have sunk in its choppy waters. But it has been an important shipping route for centuries.

ATLANTIC
OCEAN

SAN JUAN

BAYAMÓN ● ● CAROLINA

CULEBRA

PUERTO RICO

● CAGUAS

VIEQUES

● PONCE

CARIBBEAN
SEA

TAÍNO SCULPTURE

Puerto Rico's first people arrived as early as 3000 BCE. These groups were hunters and gatherers. They were **ancestors** of the Taíno people. The Taíno lived in small villages and farmed. Explorers claimed Puerto Rico for Spain in 1493. The Spanish brought illnesses that wiped out nearly all the Taíno.

THE LAND OF THE BRAVE LORD

The Taíno called Puerto Rico *Borinquén*. This name means "the land of the brave lord." Many Puerto Ricans today call themselves Boricuas or Borinqueños.

The Spanish ruled Puerto Rico for almost 400 years. In the 1700s, they built **plantations** to grow sugarcane, coffee, and other crops. They brought **enslaved** people from Africa to work the land. In 1898, the U.S. took control of Puerto Rico after the **Spanish-American War**. Puerto Rico became a commonwealth in 1952.

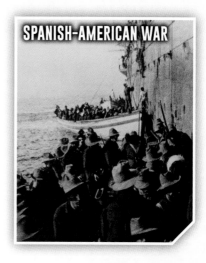

SPANISH-AMERICAN WAR

NATIVE PEOPLES OF PUERTO RICO

TAÍNO

Present-day Puerto Rico was home to the Taíno for centuries. Many Puerto Ricans today are related to the Taíno.

- Original lands across the island
- No Taíno lands are left in Puerto Rico, but around 6 in 10 Puerto Ricans have some Taíno ancestry

Mountains and hills make up much of Puerto Rico's landscape. The Cordillera Central is a mountain range that runs from east to west across the island's middle. Northwest of these peaks are hills and caves. Rain forest covers parts of the northeastern area. South of San Juan, Puerto Rico's valleys have farms and towns. Southern Puerto Rico has dry forests. Lowlands and beaches ring Puerto Rico's edges.

CORDILLERA CENTRAL
RAIN FOREST
DRY FOREST

N
W + E
S

CORDILLERA CENTRAL

SPRING
HIGH: 86°F (30°C)
LOW: 74°F (23°C)

SUMMER
HIGH: 89°F (32°C)
LOW: 78°F (26°C)

FALL
HIGH: 88°F (31°C)
LOW: 77°F (25°C)

WINTER
HIGH: 83°F (28°C)
LOW: 72°F (22°C)

°F = degrees Fahrenheit
°C = degrees Celsius

PUERTO RICO'S CHALLENGE: CLIMATE CHANGE

Climate change is causing stronger hurricanes to hit Puerto Rico. In 2017, Hurricane Maria dumped three months' worth of rain on the island in just one day. Storms like Maria create flooding and landslides. These can cause many deaths.

Puerto Rico has a **tropical** climate. Temperatures do not change much during the year. Rain falls all year long, but it is heaviest between May and December. **Hurricanes** are a frequent danger.

ATLANTIC GHOST CRAB

GROUND IGUANA

HAWKSBILL TURTLE

COMMON COQUÍ

Many kinds of animals make their homes in Puerto Rico. Along the coastline, ghost crabs come out at night to feed on clams, plants, and insects. Princess parrotfish, bananafish, and hawksbill turtles swim in the **coral reefs** as brown pelicans fly above. Jellyfish, corals, and sea stars also live off the coasts.

Tiny coquí frogs call loudly to each other in the evenings. Ground iguanas make their nests on Mona Island. They share the land with red-footed boobies. Other birds include the Adelaide's warbler and the Puerto Rican lizard cuckoo.

RED-FOOTED BOOBY

FAR FROM HOME

Rhesus macaques are monkeys from southeast Asia. In 1938, scientists brought over 400 macaques to Cayo Santiago. Around 1,700 live on the island today. Scientists from around the world visit to study them.

PRINCESS PARROTFISH

Life Span: about 5 years
Status: least concern

princess parrotfish range = ■

LEAST CONCERN	NEAR THREATENED	VULNERABLE	ENDANGERED	CRITICALLY ENDANGERED	EXTINCT IN THE WILD	EXTINCT

Over 3 million people live in Puerto Rico. The island is more crowded than most U.S. states. Almost all Puerto Ricans live in or near cities. The biggest city is San Juan, with around 2.4 million residents in the area.

PUERTO RICO'S FUTURE: POPULATION DECLINE

Puerto Rico's population has dropped since 2004. Many people have left in search of jobs and a better life. Puerto Rico has more older people and fewer young people. This means there may be fewer people to pay taxes and fill jobs.

SAN JUAN

FAMOUS PUERTO RICAN

Name: Francisco Lindor

Born: November 14, 1993

Hometown: Caguas, Puerto Rico

Famous For: Major League Baseball shortstop and Gold Glove winner, nicknamed "Mr. Smile," who has played for the Cleveland Indians and New York Mets

Nearly all Puerto Ricans are Hispanic. About 2 out of 3 people identify as white. About 1 in 10 people are Black or African American. Puerto Rico is also home to **migrants** from other places. Most come from the Dominican Republic. Others are from Cuba, Colombia, Venezuela, and Mexico.

San Juan has been Puerto Rico's capital for centuries. Spanish explorers founded the city in the early 1500s. They soon turned it into a **fort**. San Juan's location on the Atlantic coast made it an important port and trade center.

Today, San Juan is home to businesses, factories, and government offices. The city is also a popular **tourist** stop. Families enjoy the gardens and playground in Luis Muñoz Rivera Park. The Museo de Arte de Puerto Rico is a favorite museum for art lovers. People can discover Puerto Rico's history in Old San Juan.

OLD SAN JUAN

Bridges connect the mainland with Old San Juan. Cobblestone streets, charming public squares, and the Cathedral of San Juan Bautista attract many visitors. Dancing and eating are popular activities as well.

MUSEO DE ARTE DE PUERTO RICO

COFFEE PLANT

In its early days, farming was a large part of Puerto Rico's economy. During World War II, factories became more important. Factory workers made clothing, wood products, and food. Today, farmers produce coffee, tobacco, and milk. Puerto Rico's factories now make electronics, chemicals, and medical products.

MIGHTY MEDICINE

Puerto Rico is a major producer of medicine products and medical equipment. These items bring in billions of dollars each year!

Most Puerto Ricans have **service jobs**. Some work in hospitals or schools. Many have jobs in tourism. They run restaurants, shops, and museums for more than two million visitors each year.

BARISTA

INVENTED IN PUERTO RICO

MERRY-GO-ROUND FOR WHEELCHAIRS

Date Patented: 2001
Inventors: Mauricio Ambal Lizama Troncoso, David Serrano, Eileen Aviles, Felix J. Santana Lopez, and Victor M. Valentin
(University of Puerto Rico team)

NEW SURGICAL CLAMP

Date Patented: 2013
Inventor: Raúl León Ramos-Pereira

19

ARROZ CON GANDULES

CASSAVA

Puerto Rican food often reflects the island's Caribbean ancestry. Rice and beans are a common meal. The national dish is *arroz con gandules,* or rice with pigeon peas and often pork. Many Puerto Rican dishes feature seafood. *Viandas con bacalao* is boiled cod with potatoes and a starchy root called cassava.

Many Puerto Ricans enjoy mangoes, pineapples, and bananas. Plantains are a fruit that must be cooked before being eaten. They are the main ingredient in fritters called *tostones*. Plantains mashed with garlic make up *mofongo*, another classic Puerto Rican dish. Many people enjoy flan for dessert. This creamy custard is served with caramel sauce.

DRINK UP!

Coco frio, or cold coconut water, is a refreshing drink served across Puerto Rico. *Mavi* is a beverage made from bark from the mavi tree. It can be served with spices or fruit. Coffee is popular, too.

BESITOS DE COCO (COCONUT KISSES)

These coconut cookies are a favorite in Puerto Rico. Have an adult help you make this recipe.

INGREDIENTS

3 cups unsweetened grated coconut or coconut flakes

4 tablespoons butter, softened

1/2 cup flour

1 cup brown sugar

2 teaspoons vanilla extract

4 egg yolks

melted chocolate (optional)

24 COOKIES

DIRECTIONS

1. Preheat the oven to 350 degrees Fahrenheit (177 degrees Celsius).

2. In a large bowl, combine the coconut, butter, flour, brown sugar, vanilla extract, and egg yolks. The dough will be sticky.

3. Use your hands to shape the dough into 24 balls. Place these onto two greased cookie sheets.

4. Bake for 25 minutes or until golden brown.

5. Let the cookies cool completely. Add melted chocolate if you like. Enjoy!

BIRD-WATCHING

Puerto Rico's beaches and tropical forests provide many outdoor activities. People hike and bird-watch in the island's many parks. Swimming and fishing are other common pastimes. Visitors scuba dive in Puerto Rico's coral reefs.

SCUBA DIVING

Baseball is Puerto Rico's national sport. People also love basketball, especially younger Puerto Ricans. Basketball courts are found in communities all over the island. Boxing, volleyball, and horse racing are popular, too. In their free time, people often visit friends and relatives. They play card games and dominos. Puerto Ricans also love salsa and merengue dancing.

DANCE AND DRUMS

Puerto Rico has a rich music and dance scene. *Bomba* combines Puerto Rican and African traditions. Musicians play drums, maracas, and sticks for dancers of all ages.

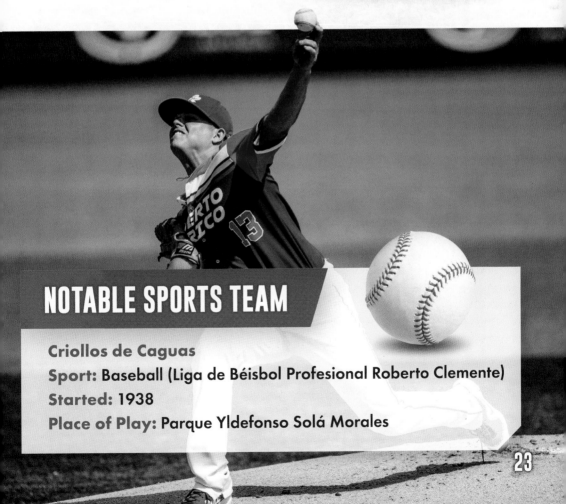

NOTABLE SPORTS TEAM

Criollos de Caguas
Sport: Baseball (Liga de Béisbol Profesional Roberto Clemente)
Started: 1938
Place of Play: Parque Yldefonso Solá Morales

Puerto Ricans kick off the New Year by eating 12 grapes at midnight, one for each chime the clock makes. This is said to bring luck. *Carnaval* celebrations take place before the Christian season of **Lent** begins. People called *vejigantes* march in parades wearing scary masks and costumes.

Throughout the year, many towns celebrate **patron saints**. In San Juan, *La Noche de Juan Bautista* honors Saint John the Baptist each June. At midnight, people walk backward into the sea for good luck. Music, dancing, and a street party are part of the fun. Puerto Ricans celebrate their **traditions** and their beautiful island all year long!

LA NOCHE DE JUAN BAUTISTA

PLENTY OF PINEAPPLES
Each June, the town of Lajas hosts the Pineapple Festival. People sample the sweet, locally grown fruit and hear live music. Some even run in a race, with beautiful views of the harbor.

VEJIGANTES
CARNAVAL

1873

Slavery is banned in Puerto Rico

1898

The Treaty of Paris ends the Spanish-American War and makes Puerto Rico part of the U.S.

1493

Christopher Columbus arrives in Puerto Rico and claims it for Spain

1917

The Jones Act officially grants U.S. citizenship to Puerto Ricans

1508

Spanish explorer Juan Ponce de Léon founds the settlement of Caparra, which later becomes San Juan

1947

Puerto Rico is granted partial self-government, including the right to elect their own governor

1993

Spanish and English are declared the official languages of Puerto Rico

2017

Hurricane Maria hits the Caribbean, and thousands of Puerto Ricans lose their lives

2001

Sila María Calderón takes office as Puerto Rico's first woman governor

2017

Puerto Rico votes in favor of becoming a U.S. state, but the U.S. government does not take action

Nickname: Island of Enchantment

Motto: *Joannes est nomen ejus*; "John Is His Name"

Commonwealth Founded: July 25, 1952

Capital City: San Juan ★

Other Major Cities: Bayamón, Carolina, Ponce

Area: 5,325 square miles (13,792 square kilometers);
Puerto Rico is the largest U.S. territory.

Population

3,285,874
(2020)

COMMONWEALTH FLAG

Puerto Rico's flag is red, white, and blue. On the left is a dark blue triangle with a white star, representing Puerto Rico. The blue stands for the ocean and sky. Five alternating horizontal stripes of red and white make up the rest of the flag. It was inspired by the flag of Cuba.

INDUSTRY

Main Exports

medicines

electronics

medical instruments

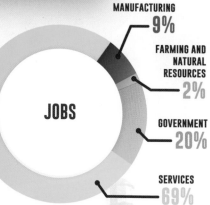

JOBS

MANUFACTURING
9%

FARMING AND NATURAL RESOURCES
2%

GOVERNMENT
20%

SERVICES
69%

Natural Resources
clay, stone, sand, copper, gold

GOVERNMENT

Federal Government

1 DELEGATE | CALLED THE RESIDENT COMMISSIONER

PR

0 ELECTORAL VOTES

USA

Commonwealth Government

51 REPRESENTATIVES | **27** SENATORS

NATIONAL SYMBOLS

OFFICIAL BIRD
PUERTO RICAN SPINDALIS

NATIONAL ANIMAL
COMMON COQUÍ (UNOFFICIAL)

NATIONAL FLOWER
PUERTO RICAN HIBISCUS

NATIONAL TREE
CEIBA (OR KAPOK) TREE

GLOSSARY

ancestors—relatives who lived long ago

commonwealth—an area that is like a U.S. state; commonwealths do not pay income taxes, and citizens cannot vote in national elections.

coral reefs—structures made of coral that usually grow in shallow seawater

enslaved—considered property and forced to work for no pay

fort—a strong building where soldiers live

hurricanes—storms formed in the tropics that have violent winds and often have rain and lightning

Lent—the time of year when Christians prepare for Easter; Lent begins in February or March and lasts for six weeks.

migrants—people who have moved to a new place for work or who have been forced to leave their homes

patron saints—saints who are believed to look after a country or a group of people

plantations—large farms that grow cotton, tobacco, sugarcane, and other crops; plantations are mainly found in warm climates.

rain forest—a thick, green forest that receives a lot of rain

service jobs—jobs that perform tasks for people or businesses

Spanish-American War—a war in 1898 between Spain and the U.S.; the war ended Spanish rule in the Americas.

territory—an area of land under the control of a government; territories in the United States are considered part of the country but do not have power in the government.

tourist—related to the business of people traveling to visit other places

traditions—customs, ideas, or beliefs handed down from one generation to the next

tropical—related to the tropics; the tropics is a hot, rainy region near the equator.

TO LEARN MORE

AT THE LIBRARY

Hudak, Heather C. *Surviving the Hurricane: Hear My Story.* St. Catharines, Ont.: Crabtree Publishing, 2020.

Schaefer, Benjamin. *How Are New States Added to the Country?* New York, N.Y.: Gareth Stevens Publishing, 2022.

Tieck, Sarah. *Puerto Rico.* Minneapolis, Minn.: Abdo Publishing, 2020.

ON THE WEB

FACTSURFER

Factsurfer.com gives you a safe, fun way to find more information.

1. Go to www.factsurfer.com.

2. Enter "Puerto Rico" into the search box and click Q.

3. Select your book cover to see a list of related content.

INDEX

The images in this book are reproduced through the courtesy of: Martin Wheeler III, front cover; Maks Narodenko, p. 3; Dennis van de Water, pp. 4–5, 11, 14, 26-32 (background); Venturelli Luca, p. 5 (Castillo); felixairphoto, p. 5 (Culebra); Bryan Mullennix World View/ Alamy, p. 5 (Parque de Bombas); Tinopat B, p. 5 (Cavernas del Río Camuy); eddtoro, p. 8; Everett Collection Inc/ Alamy, p. 9 (Spanish American War); Photo Spirit, p. 9; Christian Ouellet, p. 10; MaxyM, p. 11 (inset); Don Mammoser, p. 12 (red-footed booby); Natalia Kuzmina, p. 12 (crab); Elvin A. Santana, p. 12 (iguana); Andrey Armyagov, p. 12 (turtle); ilikestudio, p. 12 (coquí); Oleg Senkov, p. 12 (macaque); Peter Douglas Clark, p. 13 (parrotfish); Tribune Content Agency LLC/ Alamy, p. 15 (inset); Rich von Biberstein/ Icon Sportswire/ AP Images, p. 15 (main); ESB Professional, p. 16; emperorcorsar, p. 17 (Old San Juan); Greg Vaughn/ Alamy, p. 17 (Museo de Arte); Alex Diaz, p. 18; fivepointsix, p. 18 (mighty medicine); Peter Phipp/ Travelshots.com/ Alamy, p. 19 (barista); Terri Butler photography, p. 19; vilax, p. 19 (merry-go-round for wheelchairs); 168 Studio, p. 19 (new surgical clamp); Candice593, p. 20; Julio Ricco, p. 20 (cassava); antpkr, p. 21 (*coco frio*); rafastockbr, p. 21 (coconut kisses); AS Food studio, p. 21 (inset); Efrain Pedro/ Alamy, p. 22; Daniel Majak, p. 22 (scuba); Alfred Wekelo, p. 23 (bomba); NortePhoto/ Alamy, p. 23 (Criollos de Caguas); Dan Thornberg, p. 23 (baseball); Jorge A Ramirez Portela/ Newscom, p. 24; Marina Movschowitz/ Alamy, pp. 24-25; Pineapple studio, p. 25 (pineapple); Wikipedia, p. 26 (Juan Ponce de Léon); Reuters/ Alamy, p. 27 (Sila María Calderón); stockphotofan1, p. 27 (Hurricane Maria); Millenius, p. 28 (flag); Julio Salgado, p. 29 (spindalis); Malachi Jacobs, p. 29 (coquí); Ruben Garcia, p. 29 (hibiscus); E Rojas, p. 29 (Ceiba); Victor Moussa, p. 31.